Wonders of the World

Great Lakes

Annalise Bekkering

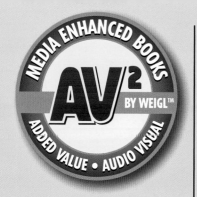

AV² provides enriched content that supplements and complements this book. Weigl's AV² books strive to create inspired learning and engage young minds in a total learning experience.

Your AV² Media Enhanced books come alive with...

Audio
Listen to sections of the book read aloud.

Key Words
Study vocabulary, and complete a matching word activity.

Video
Watch informative video clips.

Quizzes
Test your knowledge.

Go to **www.av2books.com**, and enter this book's unique code.

Embedded Weblinks
Gain additional information for research.

Slide Show
View images and captions, and prepare a presentation.

BOOK CODE

H211887

AV² **by Weigl** brings you media enhanced books that support active learning.

Try This!
Complete activities and hands-on experiments.

... and much, much more!

Published by AV² by Weigl
350 5th Avenue, 59th Floor
New York, NY 10118
Website: www.av2books.com   www.weigl.com

Library of Congress Cataloging-in-Publication Data

Bekkering, Annalise.
 Great Lakes / Annalise Bekkering.
   p. cm. -- (Wonders of the world)
 Originally published: 2009.
 Includes index.
 ISBN 978-1-61913-526-0 (hard cover : alk. paper) -- ISBN
978-1-61913-440-9 (soft cover : alk. paper) -- ISBN 978-1-61913-556-7 (ebook)
1. Great Lakes (North America) -- Juvenile literature. 2. Great Lakes
 Region (North America) -- Juvenile literature. 3. Great Lakes Region
(North America) -- Geography--Juvenile literature. I. Title.
F551.B45 2013
917.7044 -- dc23
                        2012011217

Printed in the United States of America in North Mankato, Minnesota
1 2 3 4 5 6 7 8 9   16 15 14 13 12

062012
WEP170512

Project Coordinator Heather Kissock
Design Mandy Christiansen

Contents

The Magnificent Lakes

The Great Lakes include Lakes Huron, Ontario, Michigan, Erie, and Superior. They form the largest group of lakes in the world. The Great Lakes contain a large portion of Earth's fresh water and are home to many plants and animals. These living things depend on the unique **ecosystems** that make up the Great Lakes and the surrounding area for their survival.

The Great Lakes have a rich history. Aboriginal Peoples have lived in the area for thousands of years. Europeans settled there in the 1600s. The five lakes are within the United States and Canada. Both countries work together to protect this natural wonder of the world.

The Great Lakes hold about 21 percent of the world's fresh water.

Horseshoe Falls, on the Niagara River, cascade about 170 feet (52 meters).

Great Lakes Facts

- The Great Lakes contain about 6 **quadrillion** gallons (23 quadrillion liters) of fresh water. This is enough to cover the entire United States with water 9.5 feet (2.9 meters) deep.

- The shoreline of the Great Lakes is about 10,000 miles (16,000 kilometers) long. This is 44 percent of Earth's **circumference**.

- About 30 percent of Canada's population and 10 percent of the United States' population live in the **Great Lakes Basin**.

- Lake Superior is the largest of the Great Lakes. It is so large that it could hold all the water from the other four lakes, plus three more lakes the size of Lake Erie.

- Lake Superior is the deepest of the Great Lakes. The deepest point in Lake Superior is 1,332 feet (406 m).

- Lake Erie contains the least amount of water of the five Great Lakes. Lake Ontario is the smallest in area.

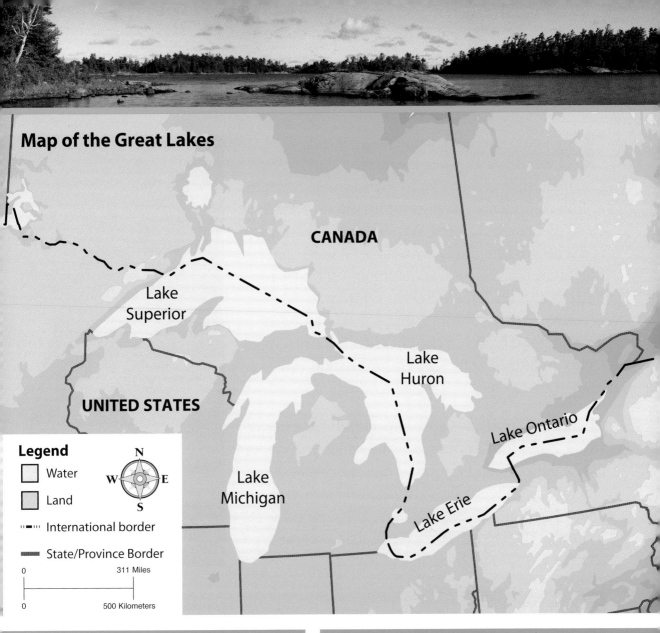

Map of the Great Lakes

CANADA

Lake
Superior

Lake
Huron

Lake Ontario

UNITED STATES

Lake
Michigan

Lake Erie

Legend

N
W   E
S

☐ Water

☐ Land

– ▪ – ▪ International border

▪▪▪▪ State/Province Border

0   311 Miles

0   500 Kilometers

Groundhogs are common in the Great Lakes region. They feed mainly on grasses and berries, but they will also eat insects.

Black bears change their diet, depending on the season.

Where in the World?

The Great Lakes are located in central North America. They are surrounded by the Canadian province of Ontario, and the U.S. states of Illinois, Indiana, Michigan, Minnesota, New York, Ohio, Pennsylvania, and Wisconsin. Lake Michigan is the only lake entirely within the United States. The other four lakes straddle the border between Canada and the United States. Four large cities— Chicago, Detroit, Toronto, and Cleveland—are found on the banks of the Great Lakes. The Great Lakes are important to the **economy** and trade of each of these cities.

All of the Great Lakes are connected by a series of rivers, straits, and canals. St. Mary's River connects Lakes Superior and Huron, while the Straits of Mackinac connect Lakes Huron and Michigan. Lake Huron flows into Lake Erie through Lake St. Clair and the Detroit River. Lake Erie is connected to Lake Ontario by the Niagara River.

Great horned owls are skilled nighttime hunters. They are well known for, and can be identified by, their hooting calls.

Chicago, the third largest city in the United States, is located on the shore of Lake Michigan.

Puzzler

Q: One Canadian province and eight American states surround the Great Lakes. Where are these states and province located? See if you can correctly identify them.

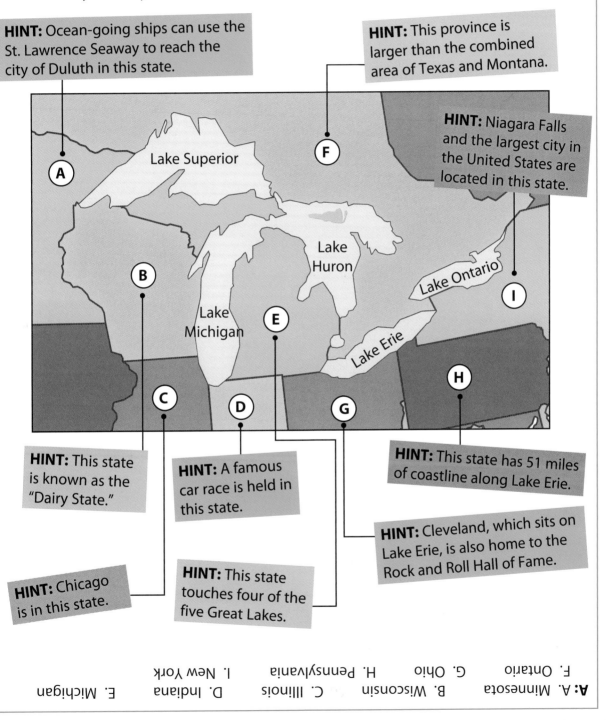

HINT: Ocean-going ships can use the St. Lawrence Seaway to reach the city of Duluth in this state.

HINT: This province is larger than the combined area of Texas and Montana.

HINT: Niagara Falls and the largest city in the United States are located in this state.

HINT: This state is known as the "Dairy State."

HINT: A famous car race is held in this state.

HINT: This state has 51 miles of coastline along Lake Erie.

HINT: Cleveland, which sits on Lake Erie, is also home to the Rock and Roll Hall of Fame.

HINT: Chicago is in this state.

HINT: This state touches four of the five Great Lakes.

A: A. Minnesota B. Wisconsin C. Illinois D. Indiana E. Michigan F. Ontario G. Ohio H. Pennsylvania I. New York

A Trip Back in Time

The Great Lakes began to form during the **Pleistocene Epoch**. Huge sheets of ice called glaciers moved from the north to what is now the Great Lakes region. The glaciers **eroded** the land as they moved, flattening mountains and hills and creating large valleys.

As the glaciers melted and moved, large dents were left in the land. Over thousands of years, the climate became warmer, and the glaciers slowly began to melt away. The dents in the land were filled with melted water from the glaciers. These water-filled holes became the Great Lakes.

A glacier is made of ice, snow, water, rock, and dirt. Some of the glaciers that covered the Great Lakes region were 6,500 feet (2,000 m) thick in places.

How Glaciers Shape the Land

Gravity causes glaciers to move. It makes them twist and slide down slopes. Glaciers move very slowly, in some cases only 1 to 2 feet (30 to 60 centimeters) per day. They erode and shape the land as they travel.

When a glacier travels over land, it picks up rocks and **sediment** in some places and deposits them in others. Mounds of sediment deposited by a glacier are called moraines. Drumlins are hills of sediment that are made when a glacier retreats. Eskers are thin ridges of sediment formed by water running underneath a glacier.

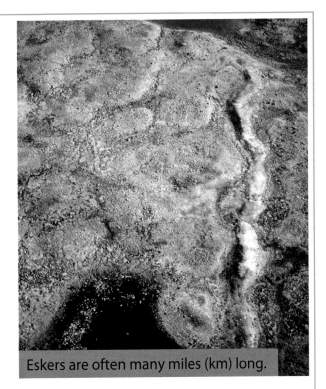

Eskers are often many miles (km) long.

Drumlins are small, rounded hills formed by the movement of glaciers. They can be found throughout Wisconsin.

Plant Life in the Great Lakes

At one time, tallgrass prairies, forests, grasslands, and bogs surrounded the Great Lakes. However, the landscape around the Great Lakes changed when settlers arrived about 400 years ago.

In some places, plants have been cleared for farmland or to build communities. Logging was a major industry in the area in the 1800s. Trees were cut down to make furniture, ships, and homes. No new trees were planted to replace those that had been taken. Many forests have been lost. Today, however, many trees have been planted. With good conservation techniques, logging continues to be an important part of the Great Lakes economy.

Today, common plants in the Great Lakes region include wildflowers, pine trees, and oak trees. These plants thrive in the Great Lakes climate. People have brought a number of new plants to the Great Lakes region. These plants can harm native plants that naturally belong in the region by taking over their habitat.

Forest-related industries, including logging and paper and pulp manufacturing, are now a major feature along the Great Lakes.

The Michigan Monkey Flower

The Michigan monkey flower grows in cold, flowing spring water along shorelines in Michigan's Great Lakes region. The bright-yellow, tube-shaped flower grows between 0.6 and 1.06 inches (16 and 27 millimeters) high.

The Michigan monkey flower is an **endangered species**. Human activity, such as building near streams, is a major threat to the flower. Such activity destroys the plant's habitat and the springs that the flower needs to survive. In order to save this plant, sources of spring water need to be protected.

Monkey flowers are said to look like a monkey's face.

Great Lakes Animals

The Great Lakes are rich in animal life. Some of these animals are native to the area. Others have been brought to the region by humans. These animals compete with each other for food and habitat. Moose, black bears, lynx, and wolves live in the northern parts of the area, near Lakes Superior, Michigan, and Huron. Owls, squirrels, and white-tailed deer can be found living in the forests around the lower Great Lakes region.

Many types of fish, such as lake trout, walleye, brook trout, yellow perch, and muskellunge, live within the waters of the Great Lakes. These fish feed on the insects, plankton, and plants that live in and around the water.

The Great Lakes provide birds with food and nesting areas. Birds living in the Great Lakes area include the American bittern, great blue heron, double-crested cormorant, wood thrush, and the grasshopper sparrow. The lakes are also used as resting stops by **migratory** birds, such as Canada geese.

With abundant water, grasses, and shrubs, moose thrive in the Great Lakes region.

Giant of the Great Lakes

Lake sturgeon have lived in the Great Lakes since the **Ice Age**. As the largest fish in the Great Lakes, they can weigh up to 300 pounds (136 kilograms) and be 8 feet (2.5 m) long. Lake sturgeon are bottom-feeders. They use their vacuum-like mouth to suck up insects and **crustaceans** from the bottom of the lake.

Human contact has greatly affected lake sturgeon. Early Aboriginal Peoples used these fish for food and oil. In the 1800s, fishers began to catch lake sturgeon for commercial use. By the 1900s, the lake sturgeon population was very low due to over-fishing. To bring back the population, the Canadian and U.S. governments named the fish a threatened animal. Now, there are many restrictions on fishing for lake sturgeon.

Fish and wildlife officers tag lake sturgeon to keep track of their numbers.

Early Settlement

Aboriginal Peoples have lived in the Great Lakes region for thousands of years. With its large supply of fresh water, fertile land, and diverse plant and animal species, the area is rich in resources. Early Aboriginal Peoples were able to live in the area by hunting, fishing, and growing corn and other vegetables.

In the 1500s and 1600s, Europeans began to explore the Great Lakes area. The first Europeans to arrive were French explorers and fur traders. They were soon followed by explorers and fur traders from Great Britain. Both groups built the fur trade in the region. They used the lakes to transport furs to trading posts.

Over time, European settlers began to move into the area. They set up farms, towns, and villages around the lakes. Some of these settlements grew to become major U.S. and Canadian cities.

Toronto began as a French trading post. Located on Lake Ontario, it is Canada's largest city and the capital of the province of Ontario.

Biography

Samuel de Champlain (1567–1635)

Samuel de Champlain was a French explorer. He first traveled to North America in 1603 on a fur-trading mission. Champlain soon became one of the most important explorers of the Great Lakes.

In 1615, Champlain and his group explored Lake Ontario and Georgian Bay, part of Lake Huron. He spent the winter with a group of local Aboriginal Peoples called the Huron. While there, Champlain asked the Huron about the land to the west. They told him that there were vast lakes beyond Lake Huron. However, they advised Champlain against traveling there because of an ongoing war between Aboriginal groups in the West. Champlain agreed and, instead, he used information provided by the Huron to make a map of the Great Lakes. Although his map was unfinished, it was the first geographical information about the eastern Great Lakes.

Great Lakes Facts

Born: 1567

Hometown: Brouage, France

Occupation: Explorer

Died: December 25, 1635

The Big Picture

Freshwater lakes are home to many kinds of animals and provide drinking water to large numbers of people. This map shows where some of the world's largest freshwater lakes are found.

PACIFIC
OCEAN

NORTH AMERICA

ATLANTIC
OCEAN

SOUTH
AMERICA

SOUTHERN
OCEAN

Great Slave Lake
Canada

Great Lakes
Canada, United States

Legend

Lake

Ocean

River

Scale at Equator

0   1,000   2,000   3,000 miles

0   1,000   2,000   3,000 kilometers

N
W   E
S

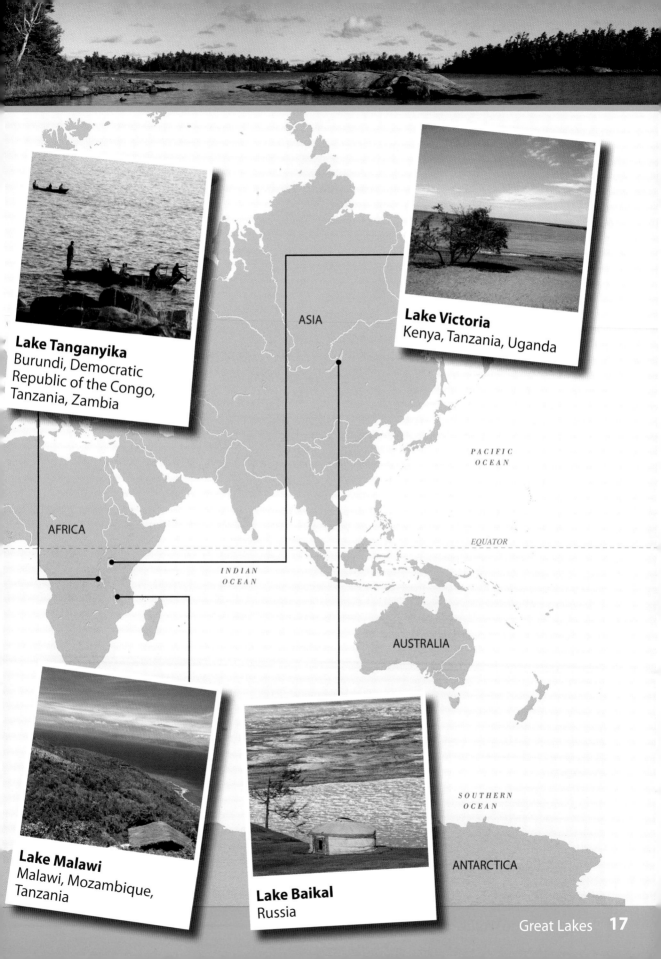

Lake Tanganyika
Burundi, Democratic Republic of the Congo, Tanzania, Zambia

Lake Victoria
Kenya, Tanzania, Uganda

ASIA

AFRICA

PACIFIC OCEAN

EQUATOR

INDIAN OCEAN

AUSTRALIA

SOUTHERN OCEAN

ANTARCTICA

Lake Malawi
Malawi, Mozambique, Tanzania

Lake Baikal
Russia

The Great Lakes Today

When European settlers came to live in the area around the Great Lakes, they learned of the resources the region had to offer. Settlers used these resources to develop industries, such as agriculture, logging, and fishing. Word of the riches found there quickly made its way back to Europe and other places. People began **immigrating** to the Great Lakes region. This helped the area to develop further.

Today, about 37 million people live in the Great Lakes region. Most of these people live along the mouths of rivers and canals connected to the Great Lakes. Communities grew in these places because of the easy access to shipping and fresh water.

Resources found in the Great Lakes region are still used for businesses. Many people in the Great Lakes Basin work in agriculture, manufacturing, mining, and shipping. Major industries in the Great Lakes region include steel, paper, chemical, and automobile production. More than 140,000 people work in the sport and commercial fishing industry, an important source of income for the region.

Huge freighters carry many kinds of cargo, including coal and iron ore, through the Great Lakes.

The Environment

The Great Lakes region is one of the most largely populated areas in North America. When such a large number of people live in one place, there can be a huge effect on the environment.

The Environmental Research Laboratory was created in 1974 in Ann Arbor, Michigan, to study life in and around the Great Lakes. Its goal is to research the environment and ecosystems of the Great Lakes and provide ideas for restoring and protecting them.

A main focus of the laboratory is the study of pollution within the Great Lakes. Scientists observe the types and levels of pollution that enter the area. They study the effects that this pollution has on the people, plants, and animals that call the region home.

Scientists at the laboratory are conducting research to assess the impact that climate change might be having on the Great Lakes. In recent years, the water level in the lakes has risen. Scientists are also monitoring the effect that **invasive species** have had on native species on the Great Lakes ecosystem. There is great concern about the effect that invasive species may cause to the lakes in the future.

Field scientists assess the Great Lakes' waters.

Timeline

10,000 years ago

The last Ice Age ends, and the Great Lakes begin to form.

1615

Samuel de Champlain explores Lakes Ontario and Huron.

1622

French explorer Étienne Brûlé explores Lake Superior.

1634

French explorer Jean Nicolet is the first European to see Lake Michigan.

1669

French explorer Louis Jolliet discovers Lake Erie.

1850–1880

Large forests in the Great Lakes region are lost due to logging.

1860s

The first paper mill is developed in the Great Lakes region. Waste from the mill is dumped in the lakes as pollution.

1909

The United States and Canada form a joint commission to share responsibility for the Great Lakes.

1959

The St. Lawrence Seaway opens, connecting the Great Lakes to the Atlantic Ocean. Shipping increases.

1970s

The dumping of toxic chemicals is banned due to environmental and health concerns.

1600s French explorers map the Great Lakes region.

1850s With no thought to conservation, whole forests are cut down.

1860s The first paper mills are established. Pulp and paper plants continue to operate today.

1960s Giant ships begin carrying passengers and freight through the Great Lakes to the Atlantic Ocean.

1970s The extensive use of pesticides results in massive fish kills.

1980s Zebra mussels reach the Great Lakes and threaten native mussels. They also threaten the ecosystem of the lakes.

2000s Serious efforts are made to clean up the Great Lakes.

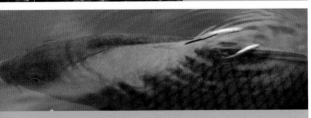

2012 Scientists fear the Asian carp will enter the Great Lakes and destroy the native fish.

1972

The first Great Lakes Water Quality Agreement is established between Canada and the United States, leading to major reductions in pollution.

1975

The *Edmund Fitzgerald* sinks during a storm on Lake Superior.

1980s–1990s

Chemical pollution is reduced, but invasive species increase.

1987

The Canadian and United States governments create plans to clean up threatened areas.

2002

The Great Lakes Legacy Act is developed. It provides $270 million over five years to clean the lakes and educate people about protecting them.

2007

The governments of Canada and Ontario sign an agreement to help protect the Great Lakes and clean up 15 areas where the environment has been harmed by pollution.

2010

The Great Lakes Restoration Initiative is proposed in the United States. It would provide funds to clean up toxins and combat invasive species in the lakes.

2012

Concern grows over Asian carp entering the Great Lakes.

Protecting the Lakes

Human activities, such as farming and fishing, have impacted the Great Lakes ecosystem. The Canadian and U.S. governments have worked together to protect the Great Lakes. Still, pollution and invasive species pose a big threat to the plants and animals that live there.

Water stays in the Great Lakes for a long time. This means pollutants, such as pesticides and fertilizers, that get into the lake stay for a long time as well. They have time to cause damage to the plants and animals living there. Pollutants also have made large **algae** blooms, especially in Lake Erie. The algae uses up much of the oxygen in the water. Many fish and water animals do not get the oxygen they need to survive.

Animals and plants within the Great Lakes region are threatened by invasive species. These plants and animals take food and habitat away from native species. Since 1830, more than 140 invasive species have entered the Great Lakes. Many have been brought into the area in the water that moves along with ships. These species have had a big impact on the 130 endangered and rare plants and animals found within the Great Lakes.

Algae has killed fish and threatened plant life. Governments are working to reduce the amounts of phosphorus that enter the lakes. Phosphorus is a chemical that comes from laundry detergent. It is a key nutrient for the algae.

In the past few years, a major concern is the potential invasion of Asian carp in the Great Lakes. These fish weigh up to 100 pounds (45 kg) and reproduce quickly. They devour plankton, which destroys the food chain in rivers and lakes. The result for the Great Lakes would be devastating. Scientists believe that trout and other native fish in the Great Lakes would starve and die out.

Should the governments limit pesticide and fertilizer use around the Great Lakes?

Yes	No
Pollution can kill fish and plants in the lakes.	Many people rely on these industries for jobs and income.
Pollution in the water is eaten by fish. These fish may in turn harm humans who eat them.	Even though agriculture uses pesticides and fertilizers, it does so to provide people with food.
Controlling pollution can help increase the populations of threatened species.	Scientists can find chemicals that are less polluting to the Great Lakes.

Natural Attractions

Each year, millions of tourists visit the Great Lakes. Tourism and recreation in the Great Lakes region support more than 200,000 jobs. Some tourists come to take part in the outdoor activities. Others come to see the sights. The Great Lakes have plenty of activities for each season of the year. In the winter, people can go ice fishing, skiing, and snowmobiling. In the summer, golfing, swimming, fishing, and boating are common activities for tourists and the people who live in the area. Many summer tourists enjoy swimming in the waters of the Great Lakes and relaxing on the sandy beaches.

Tourists flock to the area in autumn to see trees change from their summer green to the deep red and orange of the season. National and state parks are located all around the lakes.

Off Whitefish Point in Lake Superior, tourists can go diving among shipwrecks. At this site, known as the "graveyard of the Great Lakes," more than 300 ships have been lost to storms. Divers can view these shipwrecks and catch a glimpse of the plants and animals that live here.

Walkways protect sand dunes covered by native grasses, including ricegrass and beachgrass. Sand dunes along the Great Lakes support a wide variety of animal species.

The *Edmund Fitzgerald*

On November 9, 1975, the S.S. *Edmund Fitzgerald* left port in Superior, Wisconsin, headed for Detroit. The ship was traveling across Lake Superior with a full load of cargo. November is known as "the month of storms" in the Great Lakes. A fierce storm hit on November 10, sending 30-foot (9.1-m) high waves over the deck of the ship. The waves damaged the ship's water pumps and destroyed life rafts. That night, the *Edmund Fitzgerald* sank, taking the lives of the 29 crew members aboard.

The sinking of the *Edmund Fitzgerald* is one of the great mysteries of the Great Lakes. There are many theories about what caused the shipwreck, but none has been proven. The boat lies 530 feet (162 m) deep in Lake Superior, broken in half. The *Edmund Fitzgerald* is one of the best-known shipwrecks in history.

Divers recovered the ship's bell in 1995. It was restored and is displayed in the Great Lakes Shipwreck Museum in Michigan. Every year on November 10, the bell is rung in memory of the crew and the ship.

The *Edmund Fitzgerald* was 729 feet (222 m) long. When the ship was christened in 1958, it was the largest freighter ever to sail on the Great Lakes. By most estimates, the ship vanished into the waters within 10 minutes.

Great Lakes Legends

Aboriginal Peoples have a special relationship with the Great Lakes. They have created many legends about how the lakes were formed. These stories have been passed down through generations.

One Huron legend tells the story about Kitchikewana, a giant god who protected Lake Huron's Georgian Bay. Kitchikewana had a terrible temper because he was very lonely. He wanted a beautiful girl named Wanakita to be his bride, but she was not interested in him. Wanakita was in love with a warrior from her tribe.

Kitchikewana became very angry. He dug his fingers into the ground and picked up large handfuls of dirt. He threw the dirt into the Georgian Bay. The dirt became small islands within the bay. The fingermarks he left in the sand became five smaller bays.

After his tantrum, Kitchikewana was tired. He crashed to the ground, fell asleep, and never rose again. Today, it is said that Kitchikewana's body can be seen sleeping on Giant's Tomb, Georgian Bay's largest island.

Huron legend tells how Kitchikewana accidentally killed the daughter of an Aboriginal chief. It is said that silver birch grow on Beausoleil Island to honor her memory.

Recipe

Bannock is a type of bread. British settlers brought their recipe for bannock to North America and introduced it to Aboriginal Peoples throughout the continent. It became a staple for many Aboriginal Peoples. With the help of an adult, you can make bannock to share with your friends and family.

Judges sample different loaves of bannock bread cooked by trappers.

You will need:

2 cups (500 ml) flour
2 tbsp (30 ml) baking powder
2 tbsp (30 ml) sugar
a pinch of salt
6 ounces (177 ml) water

What to do:

1. Preheat oven to 425° Fahrenheit (220° Celsius).

2. In a bowl, whisk together flour, baking powder, sugar, and salt. Add water, and knead into dough. If too dry, add more water, 1 tablespoon (15 ml) at a time.

3. With your hands, mold the dough into eight 3-inch (7.6-cm) balls, each about 0.2 inch (0.5 cm) thick. Place the balls on a greased baking sheet.

4. Bake until lightly browned, about 20 minutes.

5. Remove from oven, let cool, and enjoy.

What Have You Learned?

True or False?

Decide whether the following statements are true or false.
If the statement is false, make it true.

1. There are four Great Lakes.

2. Lake Michigan is the only Great Lake that is entirely within the United States.

3. French settlers were the first inhabitants to live near the Great Lakes.

4. Lake sturgeon populations have been affected by humans.

5. Lake Erie is the largest of the Great Lakes.

ANSWERS

1. False. There are five Great Lakes. They are Superior, Erie, Michigan, Ontario, and Huron.
2. True. The other four Great Lakes straddle the border of Canada and the United States.
3. False. Aboriginal Peoples first inhabited the Great Lakes. They have lived in the region for at least 10,000 years.
4. True. Lake sturgeon are a threatened species due to pollution, agriculture, and other human activities.
5. False. Lake Superior is the largest of the Great Lakes.

Short Answer

Answer the following questions using information from the book.

1. What are some major threats to the wildlife in the Great Lakes?

2. How were the Great Lakes formed?

3. How many people live around the Great Lakes?

4. What passageway connects the Great Lakes to the Atlantic Ocean?

5. What is unique about the Great Lakes?

Multiple Choice

Choose the best answer for the following questions.

1. Which of the Great Lakes is the deepest?
   a. Lake Superior
   b. Lake Michigan
   c. Lake Erie
   d. Lake Ontario

2. Which U.S. state does not have any coast along the Great Lakes?
   a. Wisconsin
   b. New York
   c. New Jersey
   d. Illinois

3. Who was the first person to map the eastern Great Lakes?
   a. Louis Jolliet
   b. Étienne Brûlé
   c. Jean Nicolet
   d. Samuel de Champlain

4. What is a major cause of pollution to the Great Lakes?
   a. pesticides
   b. fertilizers
   c. industrial waste
   d. all of the above

Activity

Glaciers and the Great Lakes

Glaciers are gigantic ice blocks that move very slowly. As they move, these ice blocks can scrape away soil and rock, creating lake basins. The Great Lakes were the result of glaciation, the slow movement of glaciers, creating basins that filled with water as the glaciers melted. Try this experiment to see how glaciers move and what happens as they move.

Materials

Large mixing spoon

1 pound (0.45 kg) of cornstarch

Small amount of soil and sand or gravel

1 cup (237 ml) water

2 pieces of waxed paper, about 10" (25 cm) x 12" (30 cm)

Large mixing bowl

Instructions

1 Mix the cornstarch with the water. Stir thoroughly. Then, let the mixture sit until it is firm enough to form a ball in your hand and you can spread it flat.

2 Put the waxed paper on a flat surface. Place one or two large spoonfuls of the cornstarch mixture on the waxed paper. This is your glacier. Then add another smaller spoonful of the cornstarch mixture on top of the first one. This represents snowfall that adds to the size of the glacier.

3 Sprinkle a 1-inch (2.5-cm) wide band of the soil and sand around the outside edge of the glacier. The soil and sand goes on the waxed paper.

4 Continue adding small spoonfuls of the cornstarch mixture to the center of the large cornstarch mixture, so that your glacier continues to grow. When the glacier is a few inches (cm) from the edge of the waxed paper, stop adding to it.

5 Put another piece of waxed paper on the top of your glacier, and flip it over.

Results

You probably saw that as your glacier grew in size, it moved. In nature, the added weight from falling snow forces the edges of a glacier outward. In your experiment and in nature, as a glacier moves, it picks up soil, sand, gravel, and rock and moves them.

Key Words

algae: plant-like organisms living in water that do not have stems, roots, or leaves

circumference: the distance around a place or thing at its widest point

crustaceans: animals that have hard-shelled bodies and jointed legs

economy: the resources and wealth of a place

ecosystems: communities of organisms and the environment in which they live

endangered: in danger of no longer existing any place on Earth

eroded: worn away or ground down

Great Lakes Basin: the land that contains all of the water that flows into the Great Lakes

Ice Age: a time when most of the northern hemisphere was covered with ice

immigrating: moving from one place to another

invasive species: non-native plants and animals that damage the ecosystem when they are introduced into the area

migratory: moving from one area to another at different times of the year

Pleistocene Epoch: time period from 2,000,000 to 10,000 years ago

quadrillion: a thousand times one trillion

sediment: sand or silt gradually deposited by wind or water and compacted to become hard

species: a specific group of plants or animals that share the same features

Index

Log on to www.av2books.com

AV² by Weigl brings you media enhanced books that support active learning. Go to www.av2books.com, and enter the special code found on page 2 of this book. You will gain access to enriched and enhanced content that supplements and complements this book. Content includes video, audio, weblinks, quizzes, a slide show, and activities.

Audio
Listen to sections of the book read aloud.

Video
Watch informative video clips.

Embedded Weblinks
Gain additional information for research.

Try This!
Complete activities and hands-on experiments.

WHAT'S ONLINE?

Try This!	Embedded Weblinks	Video	EXTRA FEATURES
Map where the Great Lakes are and the features that surround them.	Learn more about the Great Lakes.	Take a flight over the Great Lakes.	**Audio** Listen to sections of the book read aloud.
Write a biography of an explorer who traveled the Great Lakes region.	Play games related to the Great Lakes.	Watch this video to learn more about the issues facing the Great Lakes.	
Locate major lakes around the world.	Find out more about early explorers of the Great Lakes.		**Key Words** Study vocabulary, and complete a matching word activity.
Complete a timeline that outlines the history of the Great Lakes.			**Slide Show** View images and captions and prepare a presentation
Test your knowledge of the Great Lakes.			**Quizzes** Test your knowledge.

AV² was built to bridge the gap between print and digital. We encourage you to tell us what you like and what you want to see in the future.

Sign up to be an AV² Ambassador at www.av2books.com/ambassador.

Due to the dynamic nature of the Internet, some of the URLs and activities provided as part of AV² by Weigl may have changed or ceased to exist. AV² by Weigl accepts no responsibility for any such changes. All media enhanced books are regularly monitored to update addresses and sites in a timely manner. Contact AV² by Weigl at 1-866-649-3445 or av2books@weigl.com with any questions, comments, or feedback.